Cengage Learning

Novels for Students, Volume 19

Project Editor: Jennifer Smith

Editorial: Anne Marie Hacht, Ira Mark Milne, Maikue Vang Rights Acquisition and Management: Margaret Abendroth, Edna Hedblad, Ann Taylor Manufacturing: Rhonda Williams

Imaging: Leitha Etheridge-Sims, Lezlie Light, Mike Logusz, Daniel W. Newell Product Design: Pamela A. E. Galbreath

For more information, contact

Gale
27500 Drake Rd.
Farmington Hills, MI 48331-3535
Or you can visit our Internet site at

attention of the publisher and verified to the satisfaction of the publisher will be corrected in future editions.

ISBN 0-7876-6942-3
ISSN 1094-3552

Printed in the United States of America
10 9 8 7 6 5 4 3 2 1

Tender Is the Night

F. Scott Fitzgerald

1934

Introduction

Published in 1934 by New York-based publisher Charles Scribner's Sons, *Tender Is the Night* is one of F. Scott Fitzgerald's last works. Although the novel was generally well received and has come to be regarded as one of Fitzgerald's most important works, it was less popular at its publication than his previous novels and was considered a commercial failure. More autobiographical than his other works, *Tender Is the Night* tells the story of American psychologist Dick Diver and his wife, the wealthy but psychologically unstable Nicole. Set largely in the small French coastal town of Tarmes between the years 1925 and 1935, the book portrays a cast of characters typical of Fitzgerald's fictional universe: wealthy, idle, sophisticated, and, in many ways, "troubled."

Tender Is the Night was written in a period of Fitzgerald's life when his wife, Zelda, was experiencing severe psychological problems, not unlike those of Nicole Diver. In the years following the book's publication, Fitzgerald's output diminished considerably due largely to his alcoholism. In 1940, with Zelda institutionalized, he died alone of a heart attack in Los Angeles, a death largely viewed in literary circles as a pitiful conclusion to what was once a promising life.

Like many of Fitzgerald's other books, *Tender Is the Night* focuses on the themes of wealth and the corruption it brings to people's lives. Set in Europe during the interwar years, the book also addresses themes particular to European history and politics, such as the effect wealthy Americans had on Europe and the ascent of capitalism on the continent. Largely drawn on his own experiences with the mental health industry, *Tender Is the Night* also addresses issues of mental illness and psychiatry. Finally, with a cast of female characters who are largely portrayed as controlling, manipulative, and ultimately stifling to Diver's intellectual development, Fitzgerald may be remarking unfavorably on the role that women, particularly Zelda, had in his own life and career.

Author Biography

Francis Scott Key Fitzgerald, or F. Scott Fitzgerald, is considered one of the most important American writers of the twentieth century, particularly of the 1920s era known as the "Jazz Age." The debauchery of his characters' lives and their obsession with material wealth echoed the indulgent and tumultuous life he led with his wife, Zelda, and their group of expatriate friends.

Fitzgerald was born in St. Paul, Minnesota, on September 24, 1896, to Edward Fitzgerald and Mary McQuillan Fitzgerald, both of whom were middle-class Catholics. He attended various private schools and entered Princeton in 1913, where he neglected his studies and concentrated on extracurricular writing for various literary journals and theatrical groups.

After being put on academic probation in 1917, Fitzgerald left Princeton to join the army. In 1918, he was stationed in Montgomery, Alabama, where he met and fell in love with Zelda Sayre, daughter of a state supreme court judge and one of the most celebrated debutantes of the town, notorious for her fiery spirit and unpredictable escapades. The couple wed in 1920, the same year that his first novel, *This Side of Paradise*, was published by Charles Scribner's Sons to great financial success.

The Fitzgeralds moved to New York City, where Scott worked as a writer for various magazines, most notably the *Saturday Evening Post*. They quickly became known for their wild, indulgent lifestyle, spending money faster than they earned it in order to keep up the extravagance they quickly came to enjoy.

Fitzgerald completed his second novel, *The Beautiful and the Damned*, in 1921. Later that year their only daughter, Frances Scott, was born. After her birth, the family would constantly be on the move between various cities in the States and Europe.

Fitzgerald completed perhaps his most popular work, *The Great Gatsby*, in 1925, but his reputation for drinking and partying kept the literary establishment from taking his novel writing seriously. The couple's extravagant lifestyle, in both the United States and in Europe, also took its toll. He constantly interrupted his novels for the less serious but more financially rewarding popular short stories. Increasing tension with Zelda also affected his writing as well as their marriage. Quarrels were brought about by Fitzgerald's excessive drinking and were exacerbated by Zelda's penchant for theatrics and growing mental instability. Zelda had her first mental breakdown in 1930 and would be in and out of mental hospitals for the rest of her life.

Tender Is the Night, though today considered one of his most accomplished works, took several years to complete and was published in 1934 to what Fitzgerald considered commercial failure. Fitzgerald soon thereafter lapsed into a depression of drunkenness and increasing debt. In 1937, he moved to Hollywood, California, where he took a lucrative job as a scriptwriter. However, his skills in screen-writing proved inadequate. He died in Hollywood from a sudden heart attack on December 21, 1940. His uncompleted novel, *The Last Tycoon*, was published in 1941. Zelda was killed eight years later in a hospital fire.

Although at the time of his death Fitzgerald was not considered a major literary figure, a renewed interest in his work developed in the 1950s, which propelled him into a place among the most important American writers, a place he retains to the early 2000s.

Plot Summary

Book 1

Tender Is the Night opens in 1925 at the Gausse's Hotel in the French coastal town of Tarmes. Although narrated in the third person, the early chapters of the novel are told through the eyes of the seventeen-year-old actress Rosemary Hoyt. While visiting Tarmes with her mother, Mrs. Elsie Speers, she meets several Americans who are vacationing at the resort, including Dick Diver, a married man twice her age. She immediately falls in love with him and proclaims that love to her mother, who actively encourages her daughter to pursue Diver. Thus the stage is set for the affair that ultimately fuels the novel's tension.

Later that evening, Rosemary is invited to a party at the Divers.' During the party, Mrs. McKisco becomes privy to a scene in the bathroom between Dick and Nicole that hints at some kind of serious problem. After the party, a discussion between Albert McKisco and Tommy Barban about that incident turns ugly, with Barban defending the honor of the Divers, and the two men agree to a duel. Although the men do not harm one another, the duel highlights the passions they have for the Divers and the couple's status with their friends.

Rosemary joins the group as they venture to Paris the next day. While in Paris, Rosemary confesses her love to Dick. Although Rosemary begs Dick to have sex with her, Dick refuses, and their relationship remains largely platonic, though their feelings for one another continue to grow.

In Paris, Abe North gets particularly drunk during one evening, and the next morning, while the group is waiting for a train to take North out of the city, a woman whom Nicole knows shoots an Englishman, a foreshadowing of the violence that is about to enter into the Divers' lives.

On the morning following the shooting, Nicole is awakened by a man who is looking for North, and later she receives a call asking more questions about him. As far as Nicole knows, North is gone. However, unbeknownst to everyone, North has decided not to leave Paris and is spending the day drinking heavily in a bar. It turns out that North has been involved in an exchange of money with a black man the night before, and as a result another black man has been wrongly accused of some related wrongdoing. North is too drunk to understand, so he returns to the Divers' hotel with Jules Peterson, one of the black men in question, to try to sort things out. Dick is in Rosemary's room making out with her when Abe knocks on the door. Dick takes North and Peterson back to his room and convinces North to leave for America right away to avoid problems. After Abe leaves, Rosemary returns to her room only to find Mr. Peterson lying dead on her bed, having just been shot.

Dick quickly removes all evidence of the dead man from Rosemary's room, thus ensuring that she will remain free of controversy, and as Book One closes, Rosemary becomes privy to a scene between Dick and his hysterical wife, and she understands what Mrs. McKisco has experienced back at the villa.

Book 2

Book Two opens by flashing back to 1917. Dick is a twenty-six-year-old practitioner of psychiatry who has come to Zurich to study with Dr. Franz Gregorovius. Shortly after arriving at Zurich, he is ordered to serve at a clinic in France where he engages in a correspondence with the young Nicole Warren, a patient in Zurich whom he has met briefly.

When the war ends, Diver returns to the Zurich clinic, and in the course of his discussions with Gregorovius, Nicole's story emerges.

Gregorovius has been approached by Devereax Warren, a wealthy American whose eighteen-year-old daughter, Nicole, has been experiencing bizarre "fits" and was having delusions about total strangers sexually abusing her. Nicole has just lost her mother and brother, and under closer scrutiny, Warren admits to having had sexual relationships with his daughter. Gregorovius agrees to treat the young woman as long as the father agrees to stay away from her for at least five years.

Although Gregorovius admits that Dick's letters to Nicole seem to have facilitated her recovery, he expresses his concerns to Dick about

Dick's growing fondness for the patient. For several months thereafter, Dick remains distant from Nicole and invests his energies in a book he is writing. However, during a break in his writing, he visits the Alps where he runs into Nicole and her sister, Baby Warren. At a restaurant that night, Baby explains how she is planning to bring Nicole back to Chicago where she hopes to "buy" a doctor to marry and take care of Nicole. In the meantime, Nicole has wandered from the table, and when Dick finds her, Nicole kisses him. Dick is later cajoled into taking Nicole back to Zurich with him, and within a few months they are married.

The young couple quickly grows to enjoy the luxury of Nicole's money, and for awhile everything seems perfect. By now the book has moved forward to 1925 again. Through his burgeoning but still unconsummated relationship with Rosemary, Dick has come to realize that he no longer loves Nicole. He also realizes that since his marriage, he has spent little time on his writing or career.

Gregorovius arrives on the scene to tell Dick that there is a psychiatric clinic available in Zurich. Coincidentally, Baby and Nicole have just come into more than enough money for Dick to purchase the clinic. Despite his early protestations, Dick agrees to take Nicole's money and enters into practice with his former mentor.

Things quickly begin to go bad at the clinic, however. Dick feels owned by his wife and Baby, and Nicole, in return, feels deprived because Dick is spending so much time at work. A former patient accuses him of seducing her daughter, an accusation not entirely without merit. Nicole reacts angrily and makes a scene at a local fair where they have taken the children. On the way home from the fair, Nicole grabs the steering wheel, forcing the car off the road and nearly killing her family.

Dick takes time off from his marriage and the clinic and goes to Munich where he runs into Barban, who has just rescued a Russian prince. Barban informs Dick that Abe has just been beaten to death in a speakeasy in New York. Saddened, Dick wanders to his hotel alone where he finds a telegram from Nicole informing him of his father's death in America. Guilt-ridden, Dick returns to Virginia to see his father buried.

On his return to Europe, Dick lands in Italy hoping to find Rosemary in Rome where she is at work on a new movie. After meeting her in her hotel room, they kiss passionately and make arrangements to meet again; at this second meeting, their relationship is finally consummated. Unfortunately, Dick does not feel the joy he thought the act would bring.

After meeting a few more times, Dick realizes that Rosemary no longer idolizes him and may in fact be in love with another man. Ignoring a note from Rosemary asking him to return to her room, Dick proceeds to get drunk with Collis Clay, a young Yale graduate and acquaintance of Rosemary. At a cabaret, Dick picks a fight with the orchestra leader and later fights with a cabdriver and is taken into police custody where he punches a man who turns out to be a detective. From prison, Dick must call Baby Warren to rescue him.

Bruised, battered, and well on his way to becoming a lonely drunk, Dick is sedated at the end of Book Two by a doctor as Baby smugly watches over him.

Media Adaptations

- In 1955, *Tender Is the Night* was adapted as an hour-long television special, starring Mercedes McCambridge as Nicole Diver. In 1962, the novel was adapted as a Hollywood film by Henry King. Produced by Twentieth Century Fox Studios, the film stars Jennifer Jones, Jason Robards, Jr., Joan Fontaine, Tom Ewell, and Jill St. John and is available on video. A 1985 three-hour miniseries adaptation, starring Peter Strauss, Edward Asner, and Sean Young was directed by Robert Knight.

- A ten-cassette, unabridged reading of the novel was produced by Sterling Audio out of Thorndike, Maine.

- Of related interest, "Last Call: The Final Chapter of F. Scott Fitzgerald," starring Jeremy Irons and Sissy Spacek, was released as a Showtime Original Picture in 2003 and is available on video. This video depicts the last few months of Fiztgerald's life.

Book 3

When Dick returns to the clinic, he lies to Nicole about his bruises and quickly re-immerses himself in his work. He becomes attached to a woman painter who is struggling with a skin disease, and when she unexpectedly dies, he becomes so distraught that Gregorovius must send him away. He goes to Laussane to meet a prospective patient, and after interviewing the patient, Dick learns that Nicole's father is dying nearby of a liver failure caused by his drinking. Warren's doctor tells Dick that Warren wants to see his daughter one more time before he dies.

Through a series of botched communications, the news of her father's sickness mistakenly reaches Nicole, who immediately rushes to Laussane to be with her father. However, by the time Nicole arrives, the father has left the hospital on his own. The couple returns to the clinic, and soon thereafter a patient complains of liquor on Dick's breath. Dick and Gregorovius decide that it is best for Dick to leave the clinic, and Gregorovius makes arrangements to buy Dick out of his stake in the clinic.

Dick and his family travel through Europe and eventually return to the villa where several incidents take place that further highlight Dick's decline. For instance, Dick accuses a cook of stealing wine, but when the cook retaliates by calling him a drunk, the Divers must pay the woman off to get rid of her. On board T. F. Golding's yacht during a party to which Dick had invited himself and Nicole, he insults Lady Caroline Sibly-Biers, and the host of the party must step in to save the situation. On the deck of the yacht, Nicole tries to talk to Dick, but Dick interjects by accusing her of ruining him, and he grabs both of her wrists and suggests that they end it all right then and there by jumping overboard. This is the last straw for Nicole.

Later in the week, when Nicole and Dick go down to the beach together to look for their children, they notice Rosemary swimming. Dick swims out to show off for Rosemary, and in one of the book's most pathetic scenes, he tries several times to perform a stunt by lifting a man on his shoulders while waterskiing. Rosemary watches him make a fool of himself, an act that spells the definitive end of her infatuation with him. On the beach, an interaction with Rosemary forces Nicole to walk away from her husband definitively, and she sets off to seduce Barban, whom she had met again at the party on the yacht, with a letter.

The next day, while Dick is off following Rosemary to Provence, Nicole and Barban make love at a nearby hotel. The next day, Barban confronts Dick about Nicole, and the three of them go to a café where Barban declares that Nicole loves him and wants a divorce. Without arguing, Dick quietly agrees and simply walks away.

After spending a day with the children, Dick leaves Nicole a note, makes a final gesture of farewell to the beach, and leaves for America. He tries to settle down in upstate New York, near his boyhood home, but scandals and questionable situations shadow him wherever he goes. After moving from one small town to another, he quietly disappears.

Characters

Tommy Barban

Half-American, half-European, Tommy Barban is a mercenary soldier with few refined qualities. Without the social or cultural sophistication of the Divers or their other friends, Barban relies on his decisiveness and self-confidence to get by. Barban is introduced as one of Dick and Nicole Divers' devout friends. In fact, early on, Barban even fights a duel to defend the honor of the Divers. As the plot develops, however, it becomes clear that Barban loves Nicole, and by the end of novel he has successfully taken her away from Dick. He is portrayed by Fitzgerald as a man who knows what he wants, and when it comes time to take Nicole, he does so decisively and without qualms.

Luis Campion

Luis Campion is the effeminate friend of the McKiscos who informs Rosemary Hoyt, at 3 a.m., of the duel that is about to take place between Albert McKisco and Tommy Barbaran.

Prince Chillicheff

A character noted only in passing, Prince

Chillicheff is the Russian prince whom Tommy Barban rescues from Russia.

Collis Clay

Collis Clay is a young graduate of Yale and an acquaintance of Rosemary. He tells Dick stories about Rosemary's past, which sends Dick into fits of sexual jealousy. Clay is also with Dick the night Dick gets drunk and ends up in prison.

Dick Diver

The protagonist of the novel, Dick Diver is a complex, handsome, and brilliant up-and-coming young psychiatrist when he is first introduced. A Rhodes scholar from America who is in Europe to study with the great psychiatrists of the time, he is introduced to Nicole Warren, a wealthy woman and one of the clinic's patients, by Dr. Dohmler, one of his colleagues at the Zurich clinic, which he has just joined. Dick treats Nicole, and when she shows signs of recovery, against the advice of Dohmler he marries her. It is the marriage of Dick and Nicole around which *Tender Is the Night* revolves. Although Dick must contend with Nicole's schizophrenia, for a while the Divers are happily married and gain a reputation for the parties they give and the social set that follows them around. Nicole's wealth affords the couple a luxury and comfort that Dick himself could never have attained. Over time, however, Dick begins to feel trapped in the relationship, and he becomes attracted to other women. In particular, he impetuously falls in love with the young and talented movie star Rosemary Hoyt. It is with Hoyt that Dick has a long-standing relationship that is fully consummated years after they meet. As one of the more complex characters of the novel, Dick allows his amours and his self-indulgence to get the better of him. Although he eventually comes to the realization that Rosemary is too young and immature for him, by this time alcohol has taken its toll, and Dick's career has been ruined and his marriage has been destroyed. Utterly alone, he returns to America and gradually disappears somewhere in upstate New York, far from the Europe that has indulged his fancy for years.

Although he is a psychiatrist and not a writer, Dick is seen as a fictional projection of Fitzgerald himself. Like Fitzgerald, Dick is a rising star in his field at a young age, and like Fitzgerald, who married the psychologically troubled Zelda Sayre, Dick marries the schizophrenically-inclined Nicole Driver. And finally, like his creator, Dick becomes a serious alcoholic and watches his vast talents waste away until he himself disappears.

Lanier Diver

Lanier Diver is Dick and Nicole's son. He plays a minor role in the novel.

Nicole Diver

Nicole Diver, born Nicole Warren, is the daughter of the wealthy Chicago magnate Devereux Warren. Barely eighteen years of age when she is introduced to Dick Diver, one of the clinic's new practitioners, she has been diagnosed at the Zurich clinic where she is a patient as "tending towards schizophrenic." One of the sources of her illness is the sexual abuse she experienced at the hands of her father shortly after her mother's death, a theme that is played out throughout the novel. Despite her illness, she grows to fall in love with Dick, marries him, and has two children. It is with her wealth that she and Dick come to be regarded as one of Europe's most beautiful and sophisticated couples. Despite the air of cultural sophistication she projects, Nicole is portrayed as a weak and pathetic character. Throughout her life she has been at the complete mercy of other people. First it is her father, who sexually abuses her and sends her off to live in a European clinic; then Dr. Gregorovius and Dick, who treats her for her psychological problems; and throughout her recovery, her sister, Baby Warren, who controls her finances. At the end of the novel, when Dick's affairs and drinking have become too much for Nicole to live with, she is "rescued" by Tommy Barban, with whom she has an affair and marries.

In many ways, Nicole is the fictional representation of Zelda Sayre, Fitzgerald's wife. Sayre, the daughter of an Alabaman judge, suffered from years of psychological problems during her marriage to Fitzgerald, which is seen by many to be one of the causes of the writer's declining writing abilities, his financial problems, and his severe drinking.

Topsy Diver

Topsy is Dick and Nicole's daughter, about whom very little is written.

Dr. Dohmler

Dr. Dohmler is the psychologist who initially handles Nicole's case at the Zurich clinic that Dick first joins. It is Dohlmer who urges Dick to terminate his relationship with Nicole.

T. F. Golding

T. F. Golding owns a yacht that is moored near the Divers' villa. He is hosting the party on his yacht to which Dick invites himself and Nicole to shortly after their return from Zurich.

Dr. Franz Gregorovius

Dr. Gregory Gregorovius is a German psychologist and one of Dick's colleagues. With Nicole's money, Dick opens up a clinic with Gregorovius, but when Dick begins to lose control of his drinking and patients begin to complain, Gregorovius buys the clinic from him.

Rosemary Hoyt

Rosemary Hoyt is the successful seventeen-year-old film actress with whom Dick Diver has an affair. Only seventeen when she first meets the Divers, she is vacationing with her mother and taking a break from just having starred in the Hollywood hit *Daddy's Girl*. It is Rosemary who immediately falls for Dick, and it is her mother who urges her to follow through on her feelings. Although she maintains a cordial and even respectful relationship with Nicole during her affair with Dick, she is, in the end, the primary reason for the dissolution of Dick and Nicole's marriage.

Controlled by a domineering and amoral mother, Rosemary is portrayed as a polite, naïve young woman who is clearly a virgin when she first meets the Divers, but several years later, when Dick follows her to Italy during the shooting of a new film, it is clear that she has lost much of that innocence. It is in Italy that her relationship with Dick is willingly consummated. Dick eventually admits to himself that she is too young and immature for him, and Rosemary likewise realizes that she no longer has any interest in Dick.

Albert McKisco

Albert McKisco fancies himself as an American intellectual and writer, when the book opens. Following a duel with Tommy Barban, he actually grows to become a highly successful novelist in America.

Violet McKisco

Violet McKisco is the social-climbing, obnoxious wife of Albert McKisco. She is constantly described as clinging to her husband and praising his intellect and writing abilities.

Conte di Minghetti

Conte di Minghetti marries Mary North following Abe North's death.

Abe North

Abe North is a close friend of Dick Diver and is described as once having been a brilliant musician, although there is some disagreement among Diver's friends as to that description. A severe alcoholic, he often drinks himself into oblivion and finds himself immersed in troubles of his own doing. He is eventually killed in a fight in a speakeasy.

Mary North

Mary North is Abe North's wife, who helplessly watches Abe drink his life away. After Abe is killed in the bar fight, Mary marries the wealthy Conte di Minghetti.

Jules Peterson

Jules Peterson, a black man, is one of the

victims of Abe North's drinking. Under mysterious circumstances, he is found dead in Rosemary's hotel room—a death that is attributed to events surrounding North's drinking the night before.

Lady Caroline Sibly-Biers

Lady Caroline is a thin, petite, good-looking British woman whom Dick meets on Golding's yacht and proceeds to insult. Later, Dick rescues Lady Caroline, along with Mary di Minghetti, from prison for picking up a woman while impersonating a man.

Mrs. Elsie Speers

Mrs. Elsie Speers is the mother and business agent of her daughter, Rosemary hoyt. After her second husband's death, she put all of her savings into Rosemary's career, and she sees herself not only as Rosemary's mother but also as her friend and business agent. It is she who prods Rosemary to pursue a relationship with the married Dick Driver. Speers's purpose in life is to provide her daughter with the support needed to become an emotionally and financially independent woman, experienced in the ways of the world—no matter the cost to the people around her.

Maria Wallis

Maria Wallis snubs Nicole at the train station just before she kills an American woman with a revolver.

Baby Warren

One of the more coldhearted and manipulative women in *Tender Is the Night* is Nicole Diver's older sister, Baby Warren. A spinster who lives in England, she is a true snob who makes it known at every available opportunity that she believes the English represent the finest the world has to offer. She is a woman who literally retreats from human touch. Baby Warren is in charge of her family's vast resources, and she uses that money to make certain that Nicole is taken care of. At one point she suggests to Dick Diver that she buy a Chicago doctor for Nicole to marry, and it is through her manipulation that Dick and Nicole travel alone together—a trip that leads to the couple's marriage. Baby Warren also knows that she holds the purse strings Dick needs to continue his lifestyle, and although she does not necessarily approve of Dick's marriage to Nicole, she ultimately wants what is best for her sister, and she is willing and very able to use Dick to those ends.

Devereux Warren

Devereux Warren is the wealthy Midwestern businessman who loses his wife and sexually abuses his daughter, Nicole. An alcoholic himself, he places Nicole into the Zurich mental clinic before returning to America. Fitzgerald portrays him as a weak and vile man.

Themes

Alcoholism

Alcohol came to play a leading role in F. Scott Fitzgerald's life. During his wife's emotional decline, he drank excessively, and though he technically died of a heart attack, there is no question that his lifestyle and his abuse of alcohol played a contributing role in his death. Likewise, alcohol came to rule and ruin Dick Diver. When we first meet Diver, he is a happy-go-lucky bon vivant, always reaching for a drink but never in excess. By the novel's conclusion, however, alcohol has helped to ruin his marriage and his career.

Dick Diver, however, is not the only character affected by drinking. Nearly everyone in the book drinks to varying degrees of excess, and Abe North is eventually killed because of his drinking. Fitzgerald is preoccupied in *Tender Is the Night* with the effects alcohol has on his characters and their careers.

Art

Although there are only a few characters who could be classified as artists in *Tender Is the Night*, Fitzgerald treats their characters with more respect than he does the others. Albert McKisco, for instance, is portrayed early on as an aspiring writer, but years later when Diver meets him on the ship coming back from America, he has emerged as a successful author and is a much more pleasant person to accompany. At the clinic that he runs with Dr. Gregorovius, Diver became intensely affected by the death of a woman painter—the one case he seems to have truly cared about.

European Capitalism

Following World War I, as Europe rebuilt its economy, there was great weight placed on attracting wealthy Americans to the continent. However, with that wealth came the stereotype of the "ugly American"—loud, brash, unsophisticated, and entirely self-centered.

Fitzgerald, who spent much of his adult life in Europe, saw the effects Americans had on European culture firsthand, and *Tender Is the Night* portrays some of those effects. In the process of courting money to help establish the burgeoning capitalist structures, Europeans were forced to compromise a great deal of their culture and in the process lost a fair amount of the identity that had always set them apart from America and the rest of the world.

Class Structure

Fitzgerald's world is a upper-class world, replete with servants, personal attendants, and all the formalities that great wealth affords. Nicole Diver, by virtue of her birth, has been given a handsome allowance by her sister, the executor of her family's money, and as a result she and Dick Diver are never without the luxurious decorations money brings. Their positions in society are never questioned, and discussions among friends often fall to the topic of pedigree. Baby Diver, for instance, interviews Dick on his family and wealth before he marries Nicole, and when she delivers Dick from jail, she continually reminds the police of who she and, by extension, Dick are. Abe North, in the oblivion of drink, falls to the depths of the lower classes where he dies, and even Dick Diver, once alcohol gets the best of him, falls into the oblivion of small-town America, far removed from the upper classes of his European life.

Family

Although Dick and Nicole Diver have two children, very little is made of them until problems in the marriage or other relationships occur. At the scene at the fair, following the disclosure that Dick was being accused of harassment by a patient, the children are left with a gypsy woman, and after the car accident, they are whisked off to the inn. In one of the few times a character directly addresses one of the children, Rosemary asks Topsy if she would like to be an actress, a question that causes Nicole to storm away. Only after he decides to leave Nicole, does Dick spend time with the children, but shortly following his exile to upstate New York, he stops corresponding even with them.

At the clinic, Dick is asked to interview a young man who is about to be disowned by his father because of his homosexuality. Nicole's family background involves incest. Even Rosemary and her mother, the other major example of a family in the book, are as much friends and business partners as they are mother and daughter to one another. Dick's relationship with his own father amounts to years of no communication and then, suddenly, news of the father's death.

In short, *Tender Is the Night* does not reflect well on the family structure; Fitzgerald has little to say that is redeeming about families or their roles in any of the characters' lives.

Incest

Incest is a major theme in *Tender Is the Night*. Nicole is ruined emotionally and psychologically by the incestuous relationship her father inflicts upon her. That relationship colors every aspect of her and Dick's life; there is nothing that happens in *Tender Is the Night* that cannot be, in some way, attributed to Devereux Warren's sexual abuse of his daughter.

It is no accident that the movie Rosemary Hoyt has just starred in is called *Daddy's Girl*, and neither is it an accident that both Rosemary and Nicole fall for the much older Dick Diver who, in many ways, is as much a father to the women, especially Nicole, as he is a partner or lover. There is no question that Fitzgerald used the incest motif in his book consciously and to wide-ranging effect.

Psychiatry

Dick Diver is a brilliant, up-and-coming psychiatrist when he first meets Nicole. He is passionate about his studies and hopes to write a definitive text on psychiatry. However, the more he engages in the practice, the more he sees psychiatry as a plaything for the very wealthy, for it is only the wealthy who can afford it. In Book Two, Dick engages in a conversation with Dr. Gregorovius about Gregorovius's youthful plans of opening "an up-to-date clinic for billionaires." Fitzgerald clearly portrays the field as more of a business than as an instrument for healing. Also, one of the few cases he actually shows passion about is with a woman artist who seems not to fit the stereotype of the rich, pampered client. When she dies, he is devastated, and he effectively moves to end his practice of psychiatry. And after years as a clinician, he seems so confused about his thoughts on psychiatry that he cannot even think clearly enough to properly title his book.

Fitzgerald, because of his years with his wife Zelda and her severe psychiatric problems, grew to know the industry and its practices intimately. *Tender Is the Night* does not paint a positive picture of the practice.

Topics for Further Study

- F. Scott Fitzgerald was part of a group of writers known as the "Lost Generation." Research the origin of that term and the writers who were included. What did the writers have in common with one another? What made them "lost?"

- *Tender Is the Night* was published in 1934, nine years after Fitzgerald's previous book, *The Great Gatsby*, was published. Research some of the events that transpired in the United States and Europe in those nine years. What effects did those changes have on the critical reception of *Tender Is the Night*? Do you think readers would have responded to the book differently had it been published in 1928? What would have been the differences in their response?

- The title of *Tender Is the Night* comes from the John Keats poem "Ode to a Nightingale." Analyze Keats's poem, and explain why Fitzgerald quoted from this poem for his title. What does the title mean? Are there any thematic similarities between the Keats poem and *Tender Is the Night*?

- Many readers view *Tender Is the Night* as Fitzgerald's most autobiographical novel. Some see Dick and Nicole Diver as being Fitzgerald and his wife, Zelda, whereas others believe Fitzgerald intended Albert McKisco and his wife to represent himself and Zelda. Research the life of the Fitzgeralds. Who do you think are most representative of the Fitzgeralds in the book? Why?

Violence

Just beneath the surface of the luxurious and idyllic life that the group of wealthy American expatriates lead, there exists a significant amount of violence. When Dick and Nicole are seeing Abe

North off at the train station, a woman shoots a man for no obvious reason. Much earlier in the novel, Tommy Barban and Albert McKisco engage in a duel. After his drunken spree, Dick assaults a band-leader, a taxicab driver, and a detective, and he himself is then violently dealt with by the police. Abe North, who was the cause of the death of Jules Peterson, is last mentioned with respect to his violent death at a New York speakeasy, and of course the entire novel is permeated by the violence inflicted upon Nicole by her father.

War

Although *Tender Is the Night* takes place during the interwar years, the echoes of the Great War, World War I, reverberate throughout the entire story. At the clinic, Dr. Gregorovius says that even though Diver lacks firsthand experience of war, that does not necessarily mean he has not been affected by it. Gregorovius tells Dick of "some shell-shocks who merely hear an air raid from a distance. We have a few who merely read newspapers." Much later Dick has a dream filled with war imagery, and he wakes up and notes, "Non-combatant's shell-shock." At the battlefields of Somme, standing with Abe North and Rosemary, Dick eulogizes at great length about what was lost during the war. "All my beautiful lovely safe world blew itself up here with a great gust of high explosive love," he says. World War I had destroyed much of what Europe had come to be known for, and with it, it had destroyed the lives of millions. Fitzgerald returns to this theme throughout *Tender Is the Night* and is possibly making a connection between it and the violence that underscores his characters' lives.

Wealth

First and foremost, Fitzgerald, in nearly all of his major works, addresses the theme of wealth and the effects it has on individuals and societies. In Fitzgerald's fictional universe, nearly everyone is rich or has access to the attendant luxuries of the very rich. Set in a time referred to as the "Jazz Age," *Tender Is the Night* explores how a small group of very rich Americans live and, eventually, die. None of the rich come off well under Fitzgerald's examination. Baby Diver, as executor of her family's wealth, is portrayed as manipulative and controlling; her father, the wealthy Chicago magnate, destroys Nicole's life through sexual abuse. And although Dick Diver himself is not rich, once he fully accepts Nicole's world, his own life and desires seep from him, and he slowly disappears into an alcoholic oblivion. Wealth seems to have no redeeming value in Fitzgerald's eyes, other than its ability to allow for some exciting, but ultimately destructive, evenings.

Style

Title

The title comes from a line in John Keats's "Ode to a Nightingale": The poem, with its forlorn images of drinking, fits the character and tone of the book. As a young writer Fitzgerald was profoundly influenced by Keats. While in Italy, in chapter XXII of Book Two, on his way back to his hotel where a note from Rosemary is awaiting him, Dick feels his "spirits soared before the flower stalls and the house where Keats had died."

Three-Part Narrative Structure

Tender Is the Night is divided into three sections, or Books. Although the novel is narrated in the third person, Book One opens from the perspective of Rosemary Hoyt and focuses on the glittering surface of Dick and Nicole Divers' life. Just as Rosemary is seduced by the glamour and luxury of that life, so is the reader; though, as the perspective evolves, there are hints that not all is well with Nicole and Dick and that the life they lead is not all glitz and glamour.

Book Two moves back in time to reveal what lies beneath the surface of the Divers' charm. It effectively unveils Nicole's case history for the reader just as it does the evolution of her relationship to Dick. Finally, in Book Three, Dick is shown trying to make sense of his life. The brilliant sheen of Book One has worn off, and the events told in Book Two have taken their toll, and now, in Book Three, it is time for Dick to move on.

Foreshadowing

The first sense that we have that something is not right with the Divers' marriage comes in Book One, when Mrs. McKisco comes upon a "scene" between Dick and Nicole in the bathroom during the party. The event foretells Nicole's emotional problems and is the first of many such "scenes."

Also in Book One, Tommy Barban meets Rosemary Hoyt for the first time and tells her that he is very fond of the Divers, "especially of Nicole." Barban eventually takes Nicole away from Dick and marries her.

A foreshadowing of the violence that is about to enter the Divers' lives takes place in the train station as Abe North is about to depart. A woman whom Nicole knows shoots an Englishman for no obvious reason. The next day, Jules Peterson is found dead on Rosemary's bed, and Dick must hide evidence to keep scandal from engulfing them.

The Symbolism of Names

Fitzgerald uses names and titles to add to the development of character and plot and to elaborate on the book's metaphors and themes. For instance,

Rosemary Hoyt's film is called *Daddy's Girl*, an obvious reference to the incest theme that pervades the book. Nicole is a victim of sexual abuse by her father, and the allusion to the much older Dick being a father figure to Rosemary is obvious. Nicole is as much "daddy's girl" as is Rosemary; not only has she been sexually abused by her father, but Dick, an older man, assumes the father role in his treatment of his wife's psychological problems.

The name Dick Diver is suggestive of the dual role his character plays in the book. The vulgar associations of "Dick" and "Diver" fit well with his unabashed womanizing, and by the book's conclusion, his character has become something of a social "diver" as opposed to a social "climber."

Tommy Barban, a mercenary soldier who seems somewhat ill-fitting amongst the sophisticated crowds that surround the Divers, has a name that echoes "barbaric."

Flashbacks

Book Two employs flashback to reveal the history of Nicole's illness and her relationship with Dick. Fitzgerald was criticized for this structure when *Tender Is the Night* was first published, and following the book's publication, Fitzgerald began reconsidering the flashback sequence. In 1951, *Tender Is the Night* was reedited by Malcolm Cowley and published "With the Author's Final Revisions." Among those revisions was the placing of Nicole's case history, and much of Books Two and Three, at the start of the book and pushing the beach scene and most of Book One back. Cowley's revisions received tremendous criticism, and the original sequence of the book was eventually restored.

Historical Context

Set in Europe between 1925 and 1935, and with flashbacks that cover the years 1917 to 1925, *Tender Is the Night* describes a group of wealthy and idle American expatriates who, like their counterparts of the "Jazz Age" and the "Roaring Twenties," have little else to do but eat, drink, attend parties, and survive their personal crises.

When Dick Diver first arrives in Zurich, a war is raging across Europe. Although there are references to an earlier time when he was studying in Vienna and had a firsthand experience with the shelling and its resultant discomforts, Diver is largely unaffected on a personal level by the war. Europe, however, was recovering from the devastating effects of the war that was to have ended all wars. Millions of Europeans were killed, and entire cities were ruined. During the decade in which the book largely takes place, Europe as a whole was still working to rebuild its infrastructures.

Meanwhile, in America, the period known as the Roaring Twenties was well under way. With the stock market surging, a generation of "nouveau riche" Americans found their way to the European shores and cities with lots of money to spend. Desperate for the infusion of capital, Europe was forced to pander to these Americans, though not without some cultural conflicts. *Tender Is the Night* describes typical wealthy Americans who live idly off the European continent. Although the term "ugly American" would not be coined for many years, *Tender Is the Night* chronicles the early years of how that term may have evolved.

Fitzgerald himself was a member of what was called the Lost Generation of writers—a group of mostly young men that included Ernest Hemingway, among others. Coined by poet Gertrude Stein, the Lost Generation referred to writers who left their native America after World War I and settled in Europe, mostly France, where they wrote and claimed a rejection of the materialistic values that had engulfed America. Although Fitzgerald was immersed in the culture of the wealthy and was largely known as a chronicler of the "Jazz Age," his work can be seen as a serious indictment of the wealth that arose during those years.

Tender Is the Night, which had its genesis in letters and notes Fitzgerald wrote as early as 1925 shortly after *The Great Gatsby*, was not published until 1934. In that time, the great wealth that had come to define his subjects had suddenly disappeared in the crash of 1929. By the time the book was finally finished, America was in the midst of the Great Depression, and the country's literary tastes had shifted radically. The movement of social realism had begun to take hold, and Fitzgerald's work was suddenly seen by some as anachronistic and petty. Although *Tender Is the Night* was deeply critical of the wealthy and the effects of their money, because it was not a "political" book, per se, it was not taken as seriously as it might have been had it been written before the crash.

With the greater perspective that the years have afforded, *Tender Is the Night* can now also be seen, on one level, as a chronicle of the effects the war had on an entire generation. While standing in the midst of what was recently a great battlefield where tens of thousands died, Dick Diver says:

> This land here cost twenty lives a foot that summer… See that little stream—we could walk to it in two minutes. It took the British a month to walk it—a whole empire walking very slowly, dying in front and pushing forward behind. And another empire walked very slowly backward a few inches a day, leaving the dead like a million bloody rugs. No Europeans will ever do that again in this generation.

Compare & Contrast

- **1920s:** Having just experienced the devastating effects of World War I, Europe is working to rebuild its economies and infrastructures.

  Today: After the fall of Communism in the 1990s, European countries form the European Union

—an economic organization that brings European countries under a consistent monetary system and economic policies. The European Union today has the potential of becoming one of the strongest economic entities in the world.

- **1930s:** Many Americans who amassed fortunes in the stock market surges of the previous decade have lost everything because of the crash of 1929.

  Today: After the stock market decline of 2000 and the "dot com" crash, many of the young Americans who became rich with stock options in the 1990s have lost much of their wealth.

- **1930s:** Although many American blacks had relocated to France to avoid the discrimination in the United States, discrimination against blacks still exists, and blacks have a difficult time entering some businesses and public establishments.

  Today: Discrimination is illegal in France and is considered a human rights violation.

- **1930s:** By the time *Tender Is the Night* is published, many readers and critics have come to embrace the new movement of "social realism" in literature and the art.

Today: Social realism is not a viable artistic movement, per se, although elements of the movement and working class themes abound in contemporary literature and art.

- **1920s–1930s:** F. Scott Fitzgerald's long-standing relationship with his editor at Scribners, Maxwell Perkins, is instrumental to his career. Perkins helps to guide virtually every aspect of Fitzgeralds' life, including his writing, finances, and health-related issues.

  Today: The role that editors in large publishing firms once held has been primarily replaced by agents. The "Maxwell Perkinses" of the past are mostly long gone.

Tender Is the Night is also very much a critique of the burgeoning psychiatric industry to which the wealthy had access. When Dick Diver traveled to Zurich, Europe was being greatly affected by the psychoanalytic theories of Sigmund Freud and his contemporaries. Fitzgerald, because of his wife's long-standing psychiatric problems, became something of an expert on psychiatry and its various theories and cures. Although psychiatry was making huge theoretical and practical leaps during the time *Tender Is the Night* takes place, the fact is that it was very much a cure for the very wealthy, a point that Fitzgerald clearly recognizes and effectively criticizes throughout his work.

Critical Overview

When it was first published in 1934, reviewers and readers picked up *Tender Is the Night* with some trepidation. It had been nearly a decade since his masterpiece, *The Great Gatsby*, had been published, and there were rumors in literary circles that Fitzgerald was done for as a writer. Although the book did not sell nearly as well as his earlier books, reviewers were generally favorable in their response to Fitzgerald's new book. (*Tender Is the Night* sold about fifteen thousand copies in 1934, according to Matthew J. Bruccoli, writing in his introduction to *Reader's Companion to F. Scott Fitzgerald's Tender Is the Night*, compared to the forty-one thousand copies *This Side of Paradise* sold in its first year of publication and the fifty thousand copies *The Beautiful and the Damned* sold in its first year.) Over the years, critics and scholars have come to regard *Tender Is the Night* not only as one of Fitzgerald's major works but one of American literature's most important novels of the twentieth century.

According to Bruccoli, of the twenty-four reviews published in "influential American periodicals, nine were favorable, six were unfavorable, and nine were mixed."

Writing in the *New York Times*, John Chamberlain called the rumors of Fitzgerald's demise "gossip," and he went on to write that from a technical viewpoint, although *Tender Is the Night* is not as perfect as *The Great Gatsby*, it is "an exciting and psychologically apt study in the disintegration of a marriage." In contrast, Horace Gregory, writing in the *New York Herald Tribune*, described the book as being "not all that it should have been. There is an air of dangerous fatality about it, as though the author were sharing the failure of his protagonist." Gregory, however, concluded his review by acknowledging that several isolated scenes in the book had "extraordinary power" and would "not be soon forgotten."

In a review titled "Fitzgerald's Novel a Masterpiece," Cameron Rogers, referring to the long period of time it had been since *The Great Gatsby* was published, wrote in the *San Francisco Chronicle* that "*Tender Is the Night* is so well worth [the wait] that Fitzgerald's silence … seems natural and explicable" and that "there is so much beauty, so much compassion and so much understanding [in the book] that it seems as though it could only have sprung from a mind left wisely fallow."

In a criticism of the book that continues to this day, Mary M. Colum, in her *Forum and Century* review, pointed to the weakness of Fitzgerald's characterizations, especially Nicole's. Colum calls passages describing Nicole "more like a case history from a textbook than a novelist's study of a real character." And in Fitzgerald's hometown paper, the *St. Paul Dispatch*, James Gray called the novel "a big, sprawling, undisciplined, badly coordinated book" and went on to call it "immature."

One of the issues that Fitzgerald faced was that in the nine years since he had last published, the cultural make-up of the United States had changed dramatically. In a short piece published in the *New York Times* a few days after his review of *Tender Is the Night* appeared, John Chamberlain encapsulated one of the effects this time lag had on the reception of the book. After reading the early reviews of the book, Chamberlain concluded that none of them were "alike; no two had the same tone." He noted that some critics thought "Fitzgerald was writing about his usual jazz age boys and girls; others that he had a 'timeless' problem on his hands."

Chamberlain's observations of the book's critical responses underscored the challenges Fitzgerald had with *Tender Is the Night*. In the nine years since he had published *The Great Gatsby*, the American psyche and reading public had changed radically. Although *Tender Is the Night* was not the same type of book as was *The Great Gatsby*, it was not sufficiently different or enough reflective of society's changes to appease many of his critics or readers. The so-called "Jazz Age," a time noted for its extravagance and material excesses, and the period in which Fitzgerald's reputation had flowered, had been replaced by the severe austerity of the depression. As a result, the literary tastes of the society had changed radically; many reviewers and readers had little patience for books reminding them of the frivolous past, and the age of social realism had begun to emerge across all art forms. *Tender Is the Night*'s characterizations of the rich and idle seemed anachronistic to many readers and reviewers, and for many the book was not the type of literature the difficult times were calling for. As a result, the book's reception was not uniform in either its praise or its criticism; it would take years for critics to gain the distance necessary to understand the book's complexities and its relationship to Fitzgerald's other works.

Sources

Bruccoli, Matthew Joseph, with Judith S. Baughman, "Introduction," in *Reader's Companion to F. Scott Fitzgerald's "Tender Is the Night,"* University of South Carolina Press, 1996, pp. 1–48.

Chamberlain, John, "Book of the Times," in *"Tender Is the Night": Essays in Criticism*, edited by Marvin LaHood, Indiana University Press, 1969, pp. 68–70; originally published in *New York Times*, April 13, 1934.

Colum, Mary M., "The Psychopathic Novel," in *"Tender Is the Night": Essays in Criticism*, edited by Marvin LaHood, Indiana University Press, 1969, pp. 59–62; originally published in *Forum and Century 91*, April 1934.

Gray, James, "Scott Fitzgerald Re-Enters, Leading Bewildered Giant," in *"Tender Is the Night": Essays in Criticism*, edited by Marvin LaHood, Indiana University Press, pp. 64–66; originally published in *St. Paul Dispatch*, April 12, 1934.

Gregory, Horace, "A Generation Riding to Romantic Death," in *"Tender Is the Night": Essays in Criticism*, edited by Marvin LaHood, Indiana University Press, pp. 72–74; originally published in *New York Herald Tribune*, April 15, 1934.

Rogers, Cameron, "Fitzgerald's Novel a Masterpiece," in *"Tender Is the Night": Essays in Criticism*, edited by Marvin LaHood, Indiana

University Press, 1969, pp. 64–66; originally
published in *San Francisco Chronicle*, April 15,
1934.

Further Reading

Allen, Frederick L., *Only Yesterday: An Informal History of the 1920's*, HarperCollins, 2000 (rev. ed.).

> First published in 1931 and reissued in 2000, *Only Yesterday* is, as the book's subtitle suggests, an informal account of the decade that has come to be known as the "Roaring Twenties." The book has a special focus on the rising market and its subsequent crash and gives a good account of the atmosphere of the times in which Fitzgerald was writing.

Berg, A. Scott, *Max Perkins: Editor of Genius*, Riverhead Books, 1977.

> Winner of the National Book Award, Berg's biography of Fitzgerald's editor reveals the profound influence Perkins had not only on Fitzgerald but also on Ernest Hemingway, Thomas Wolfe, and many of their contemporaries.

Bruccoli, Matthew J., *Some Sort of Epic Grandeur: The Life of F. Scott Fitzgerald,* University of South Carolina Press, 2002 (rev. ed.).

> First published in 1981, Bruccoli's

biography of Fitzgerald has long been considered the definitive work on the author. In the revised edition, Bruccoli adds new material from more recently discovered manuscripts and papers.

Bruccoli, Matthew J., ed., *Zelda Fitzgerald: The Collected Writings*, University of Alabama Press, 1997.

Although F. Scott Fitzgerald was the more well-known writer of the family, his wife Zelda wrote a novel, *Save Me the Waltz*, and many stories and poems, some of which were published during her life. Bruccoli's collection brings these writings together and helps to round out Zelda's character.

Milford, Nancy, *Zelda: A Biography*, HarperPerennial, 2001 (rev. ed.).

Based on the author's doctoral dissertation, the book offers the most complete picture of Zelda Fitzgerald from her youth as a southern belle through her tumultuous marriage to Fitzgerald, and to her death in a sanatorium fire.

Wheelock, John Hall, *Editor to Author: The Letters of Maxwell Perkins*, Charles Scribner's Sons, 1987.

Taken as a whole, the letters by

Fitzgerald's editor, Maxwell Perkins, show the profound love and respect Perkins had not only for his writers but for literature in general. Perkins's relationship with Fitzgerald is revealed in dozens of letters he wrote to him, or about him, over the years.

Lightning Source UK Ltd.
Milton Keynes UK
UKHW021501280622
405074UK00009B/511